BIG·NOTE
CONTEMPORARY
POPHITS

ISBN 0-634-01423-4

HAL•LEONARD®
CORPORATION
7777 W. BLUEMOUND RD. P.O. BOX 13819 MILWAUKEE, WI 53213

Visit Hal Leonard Online at
www.halleonard.com

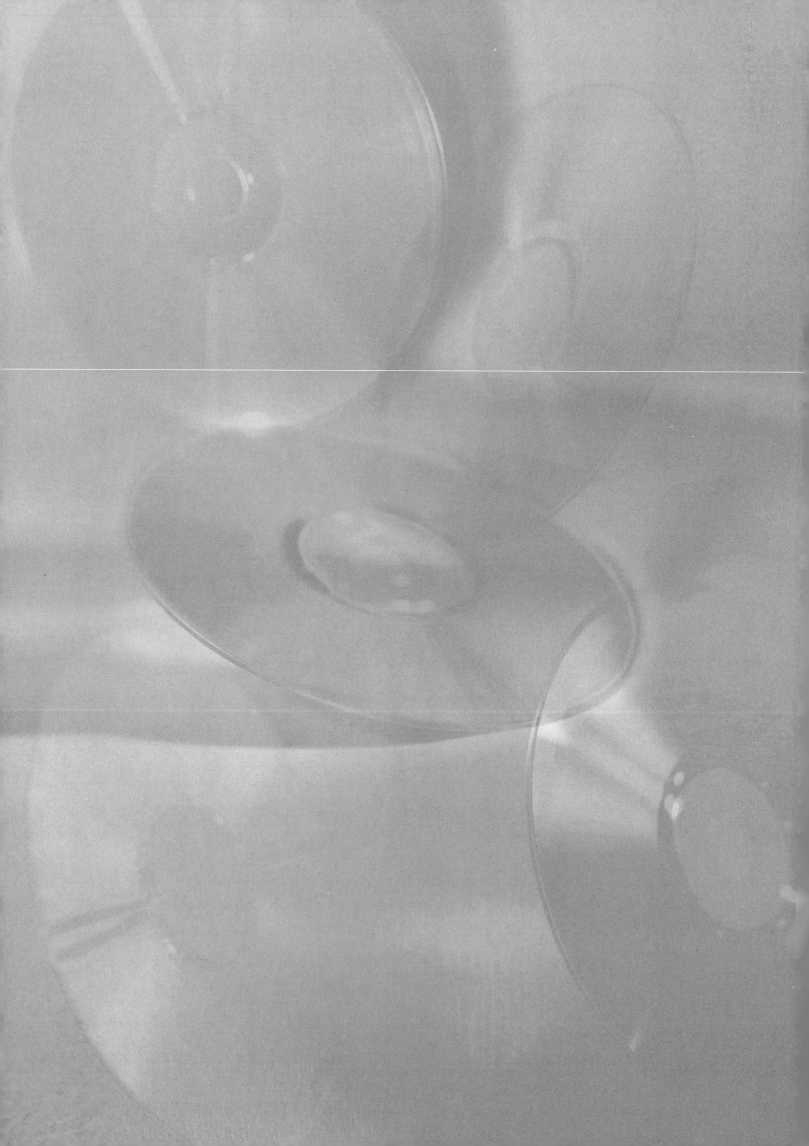

CONTENTS

ALL MY LIFE

Words by JOEL HAILEY
Music by JOEL HAILEY and RORY BENNETT

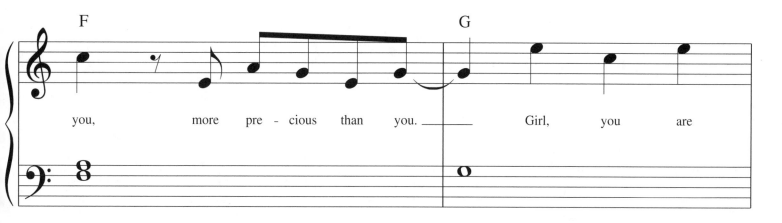

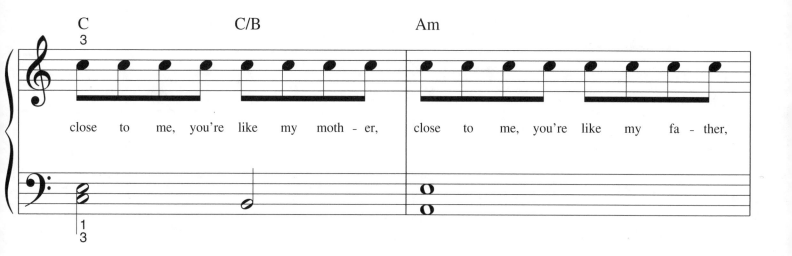

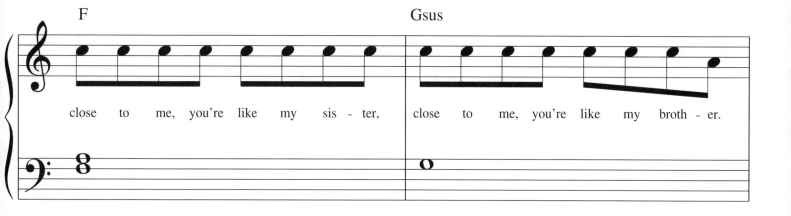

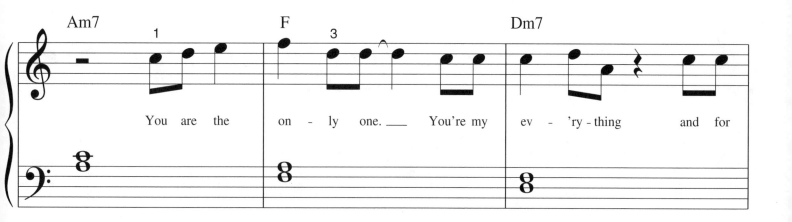

6

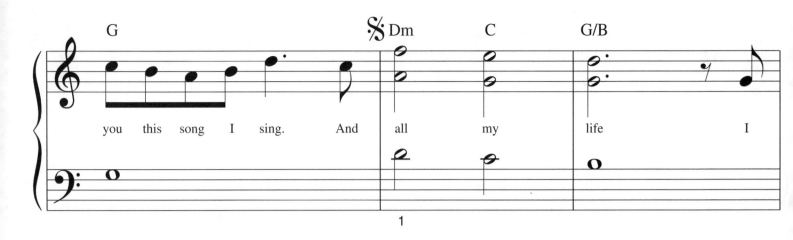

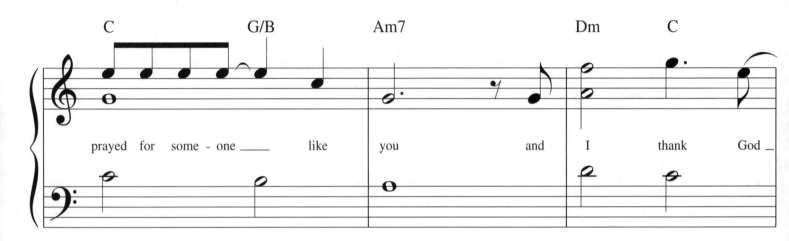

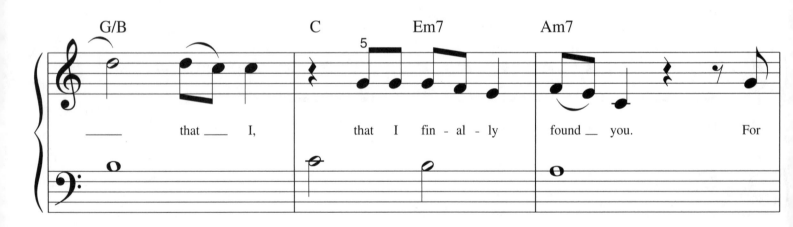

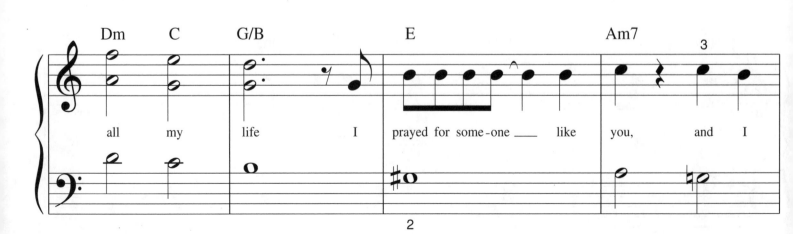

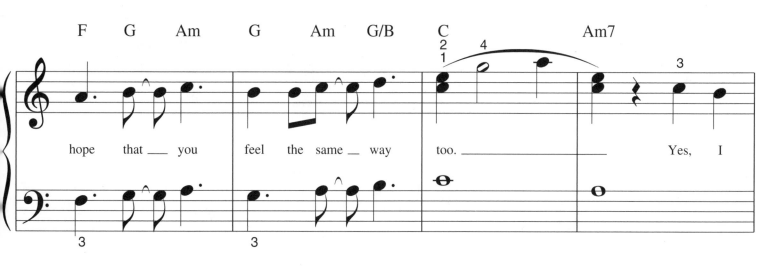

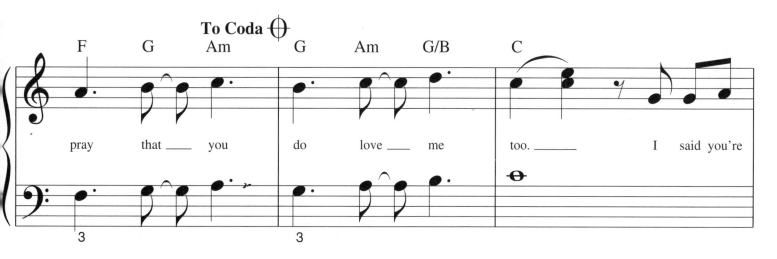

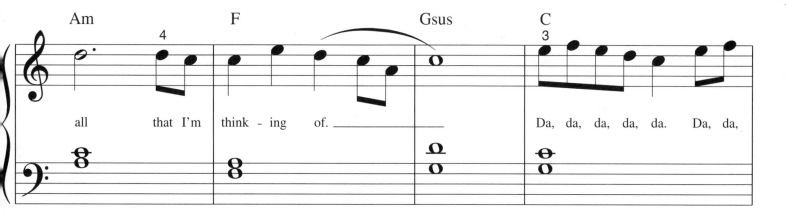

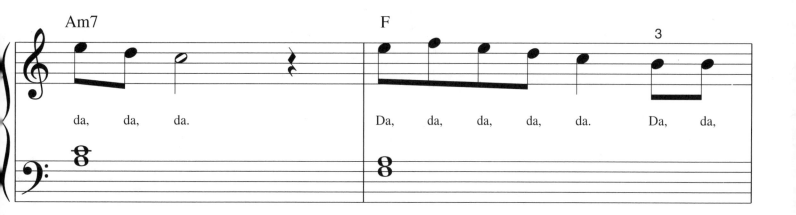

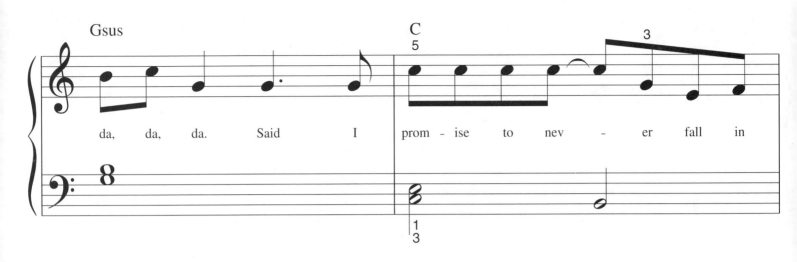

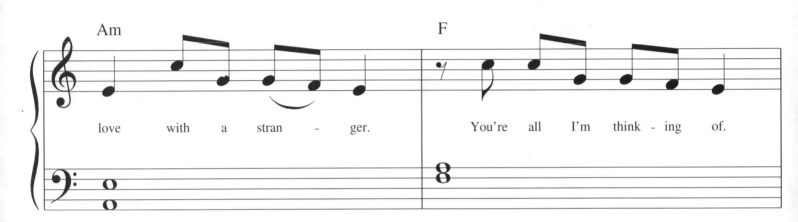

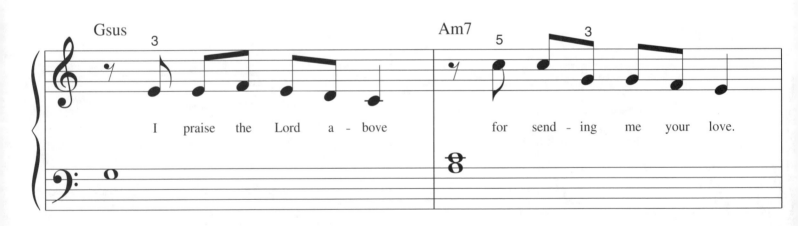

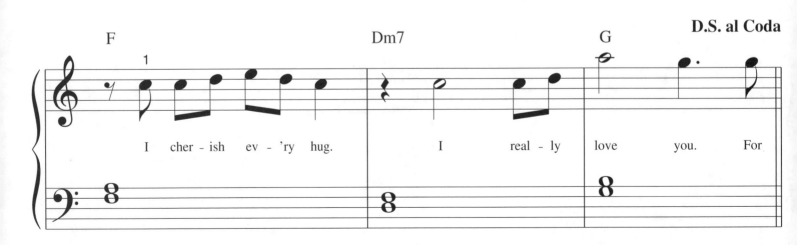

CODA

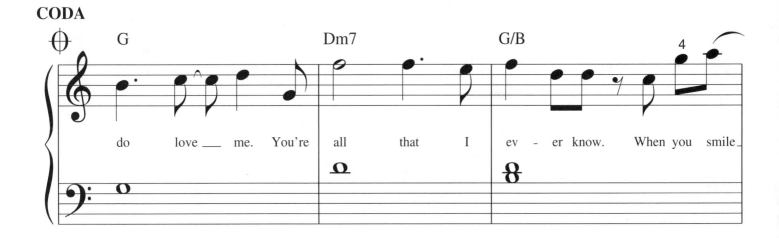

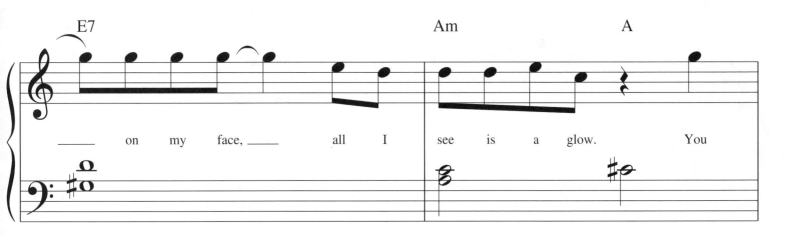

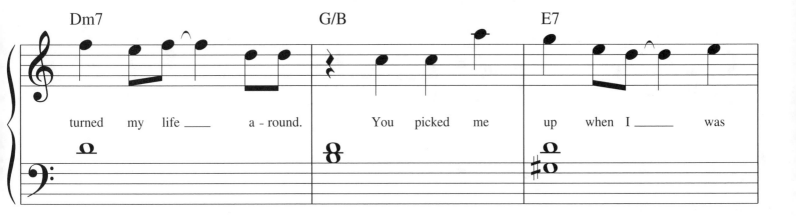

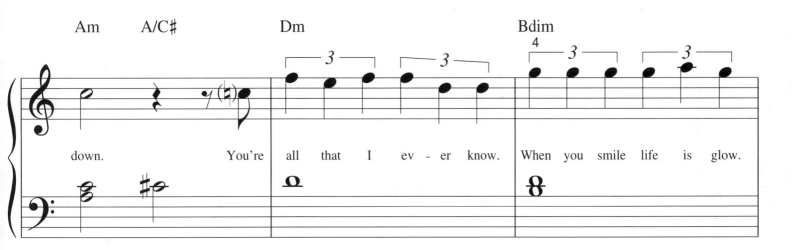

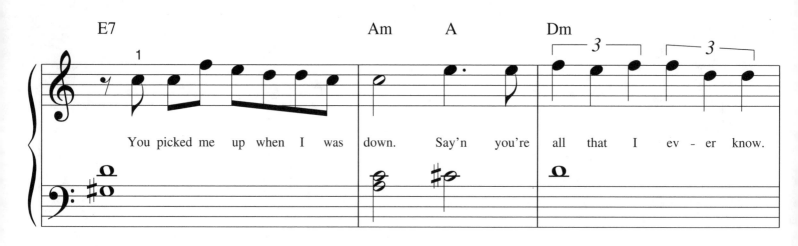

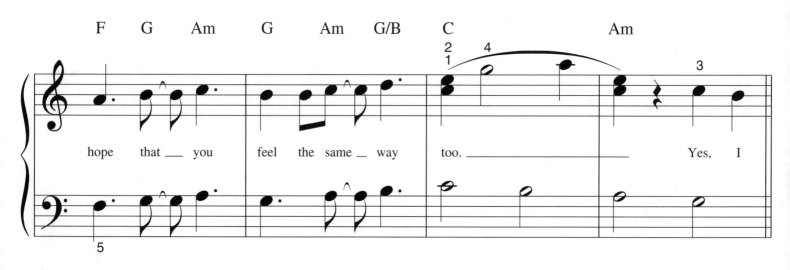

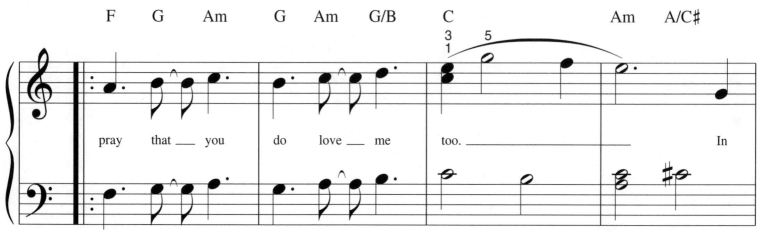

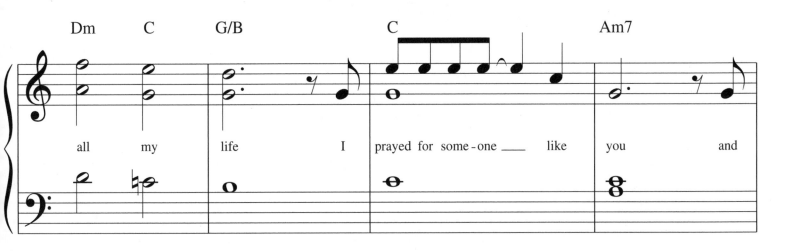

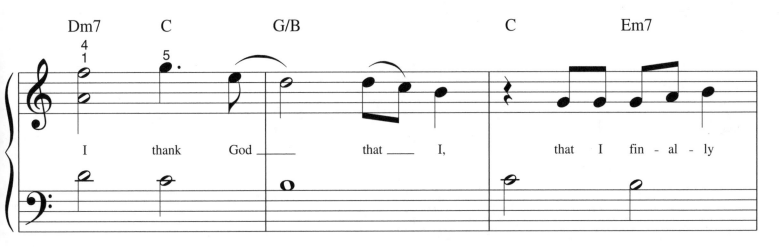

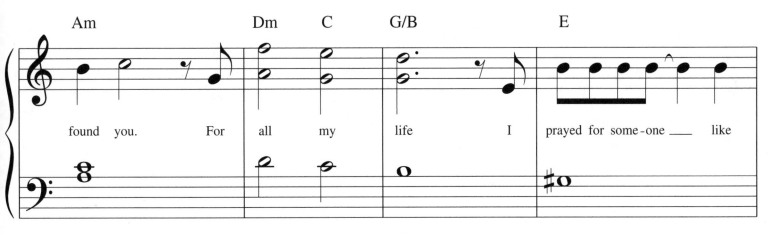

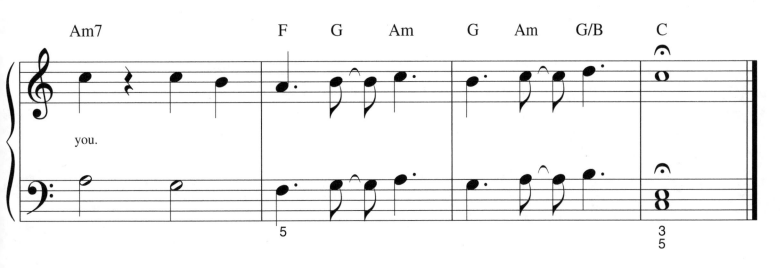

ANGEL

Words and Music by
SARAH McLACHLAN

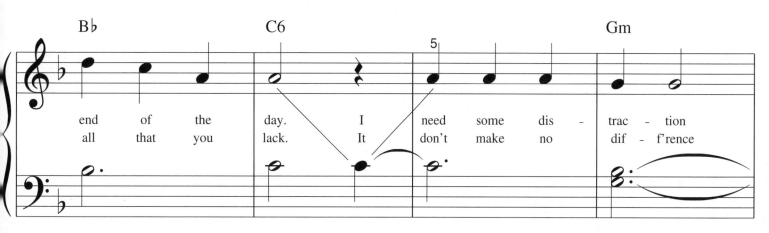

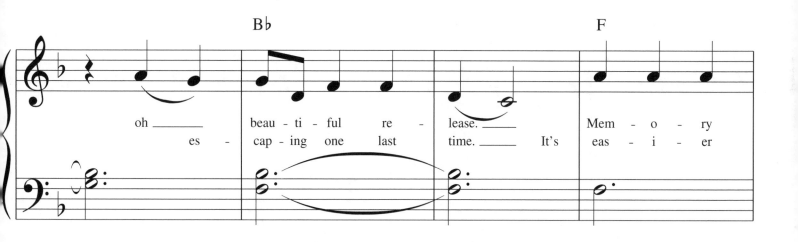

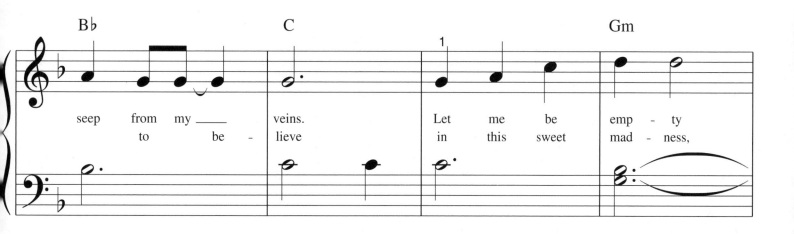

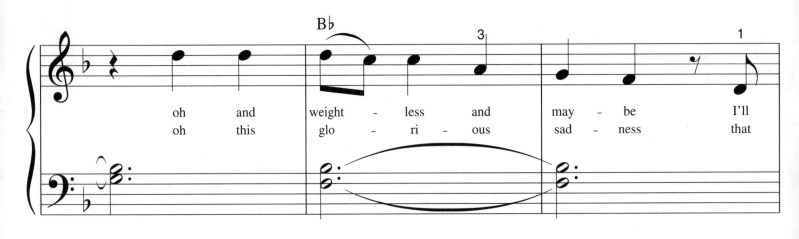

oh and weight - less and may - be I'll
oh this glo - ri - ous sad - ness that

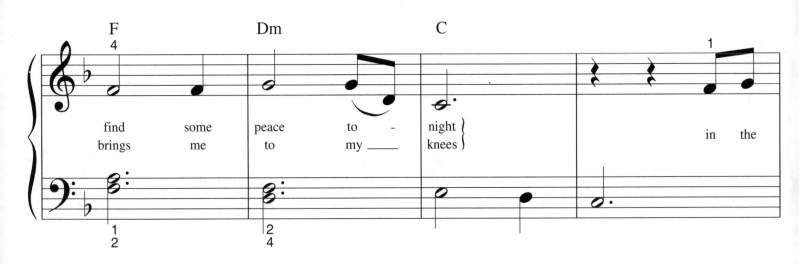

find some peace to - night
brings me to my knees in the

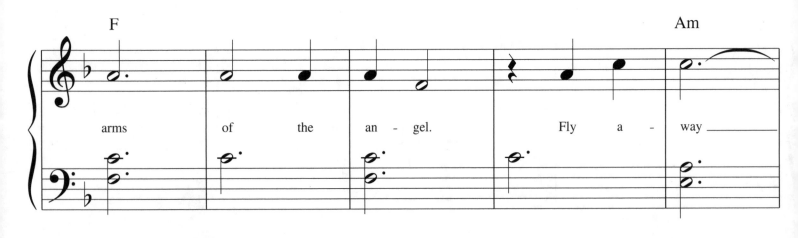

arms of the an - gel. Fly a - way

from here, from this dark cold ho -

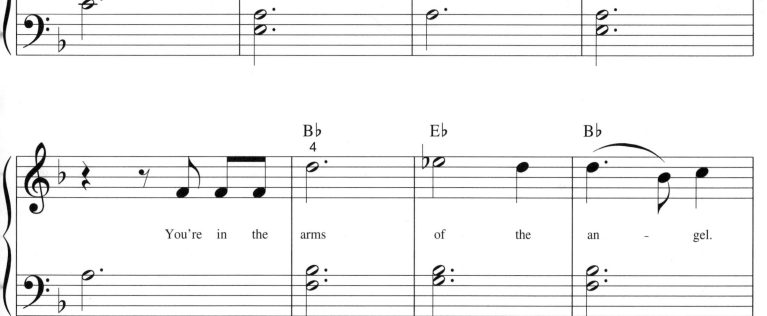

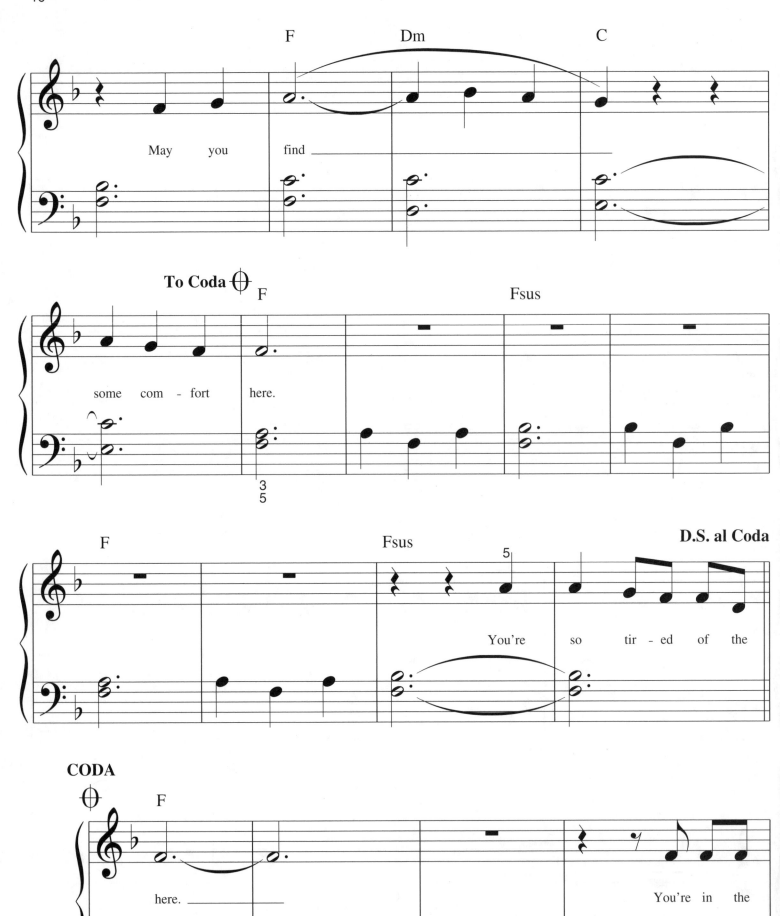

COLORS OF THE WIND

from Walt Disney's POCAHONTAS

Music by ALAN MENKEN
Lyrics by STEPHEN SCHWARTZ

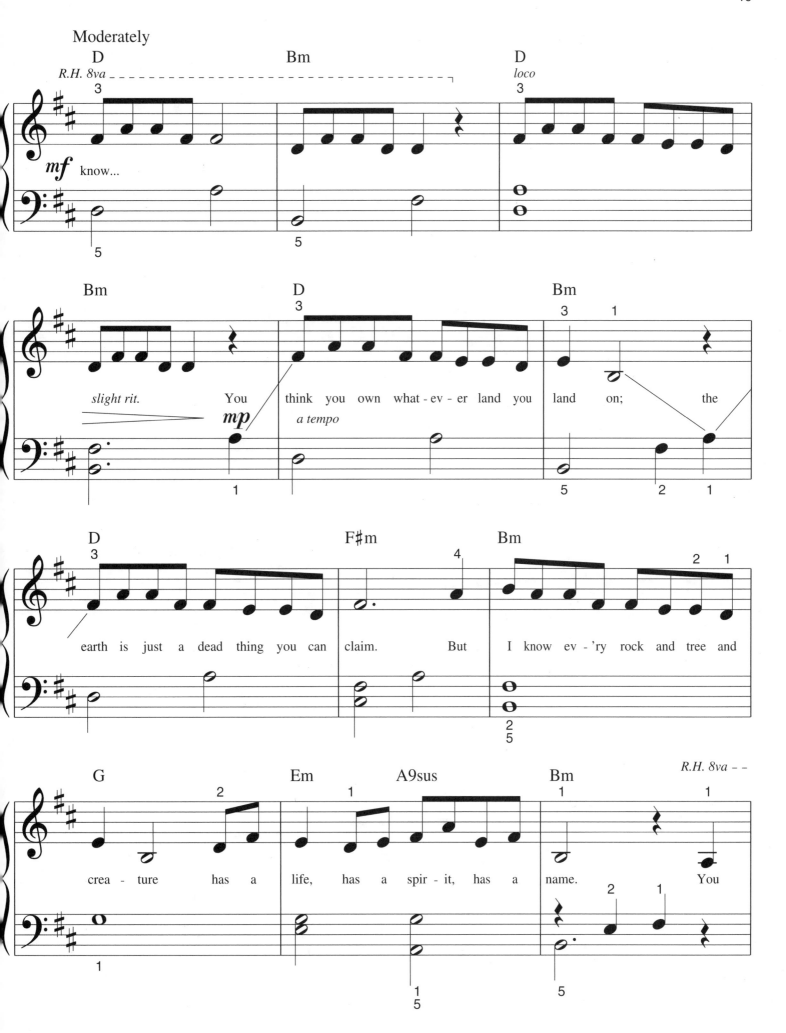

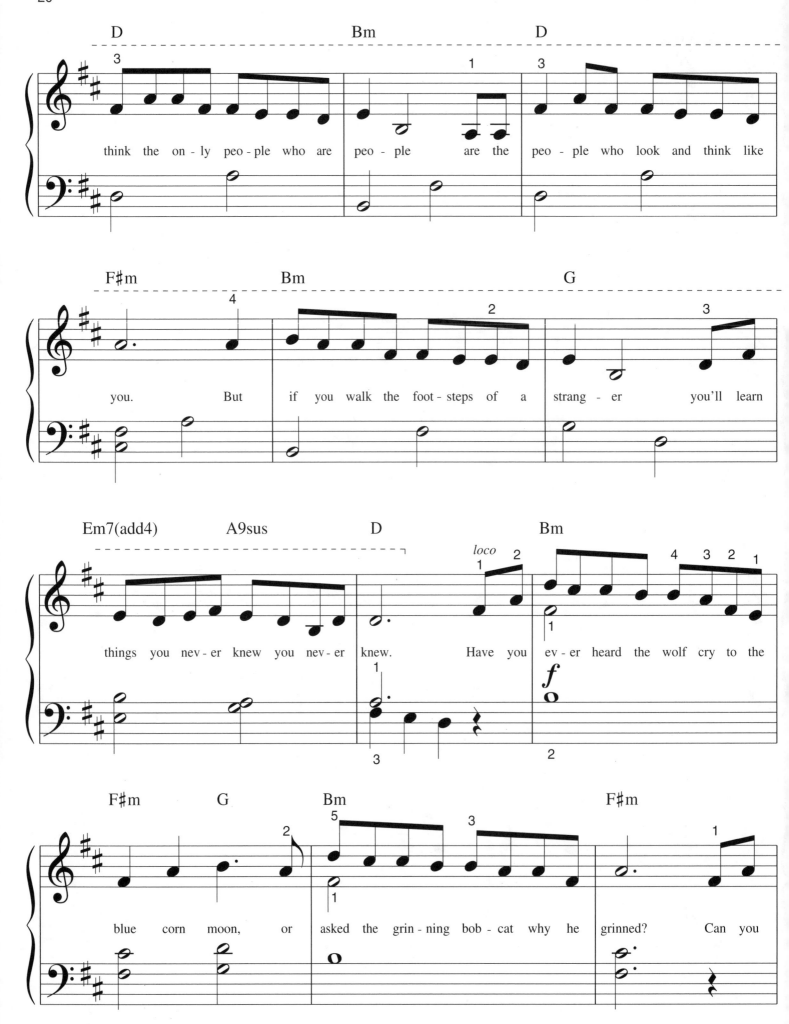

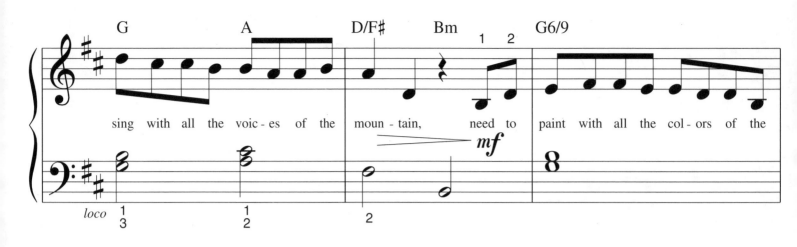

sing with all the voic - es of the moun - tain, need to paint with all the col - ors of the

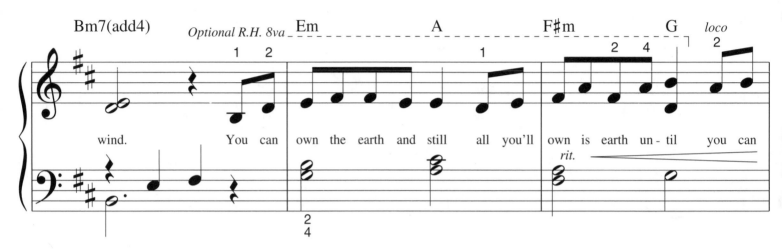

wind. You can own the earth and still all you'll own is earth un - til you can

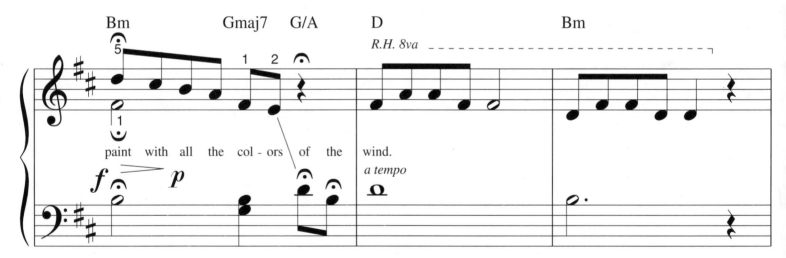

paint with all the col - ors of the wind.

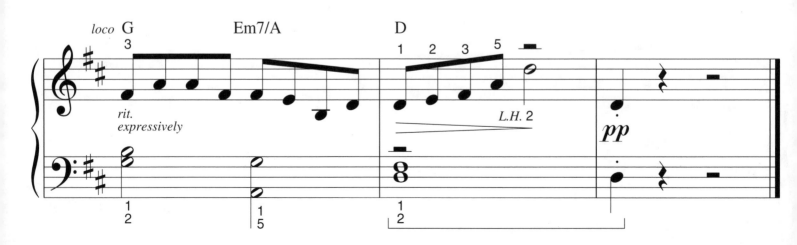

I WILL REMEMBER YOU
Theme from THE BROTHERS McMULLEN

Words and Music by SARAH McLACHLAN,
SEAMUS EGAN and DAVE MERENDA

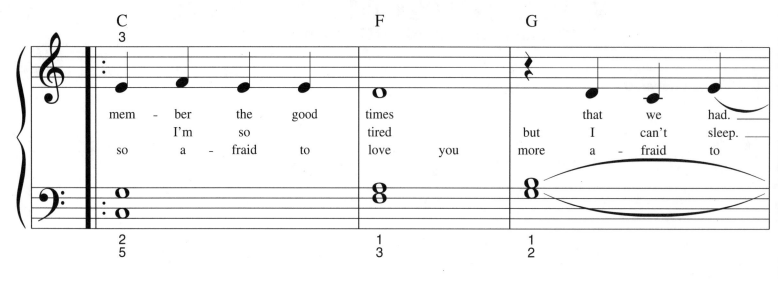

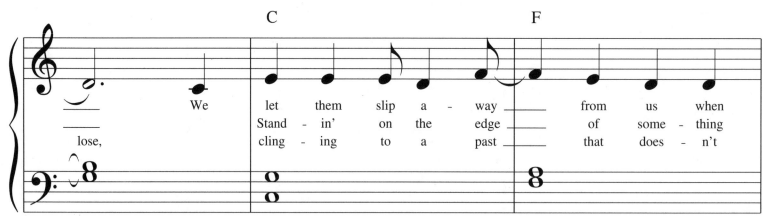

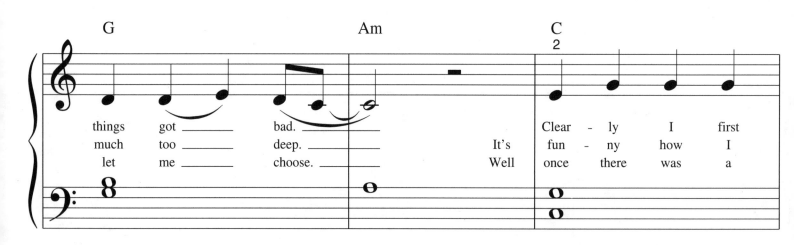

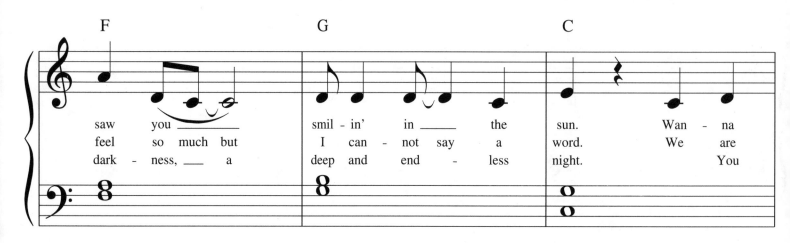

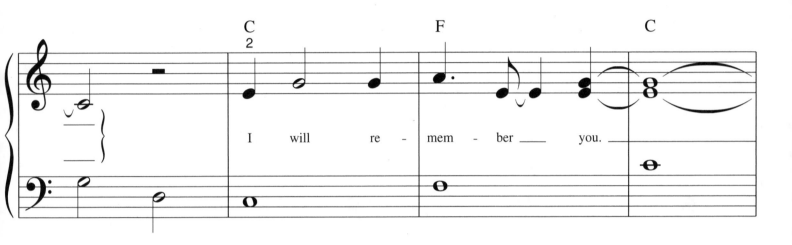

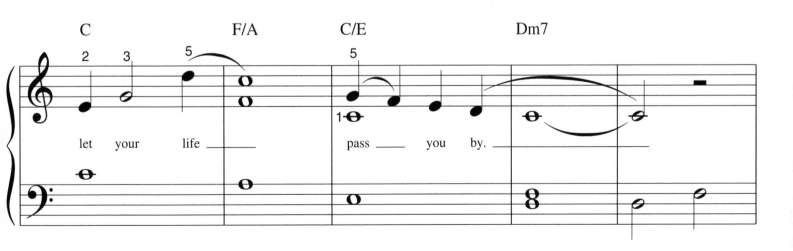

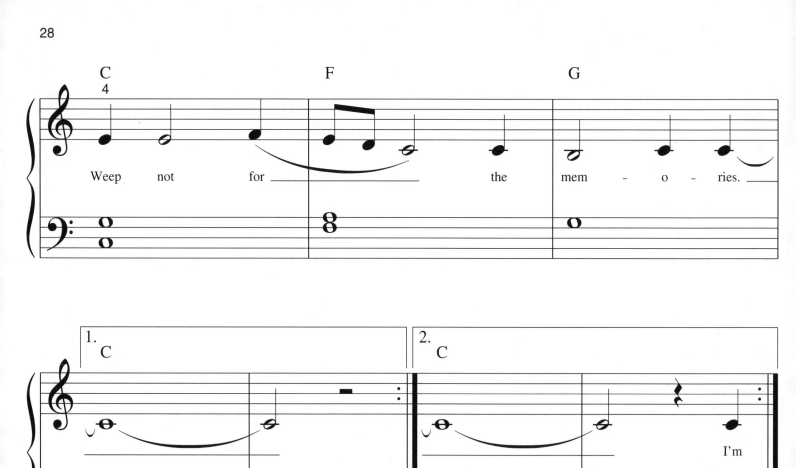

Weep not for ____ the mem - o - ries.

I'm

I will re - mem - ber ____ you.

Will you re - mem - ber ____ me?

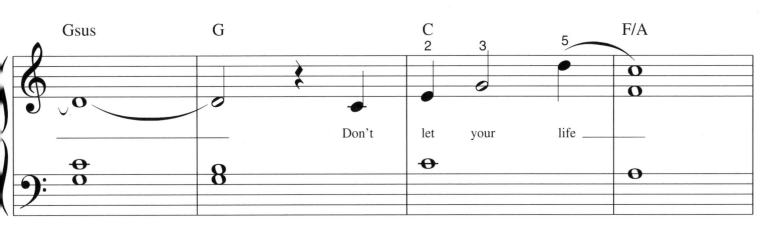

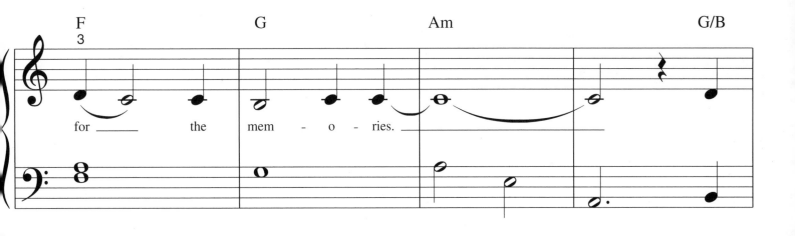

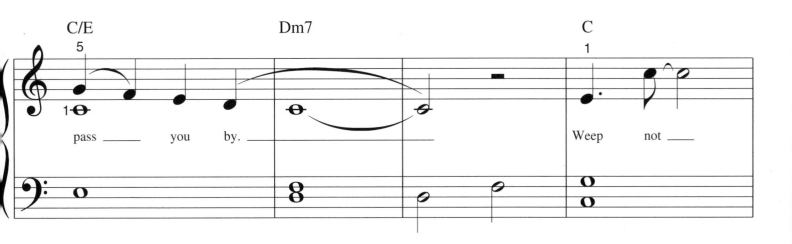

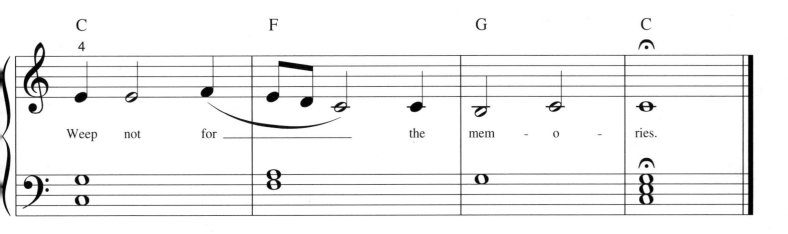

I'LL BE

Words and Music by
EDWIN McCAIN

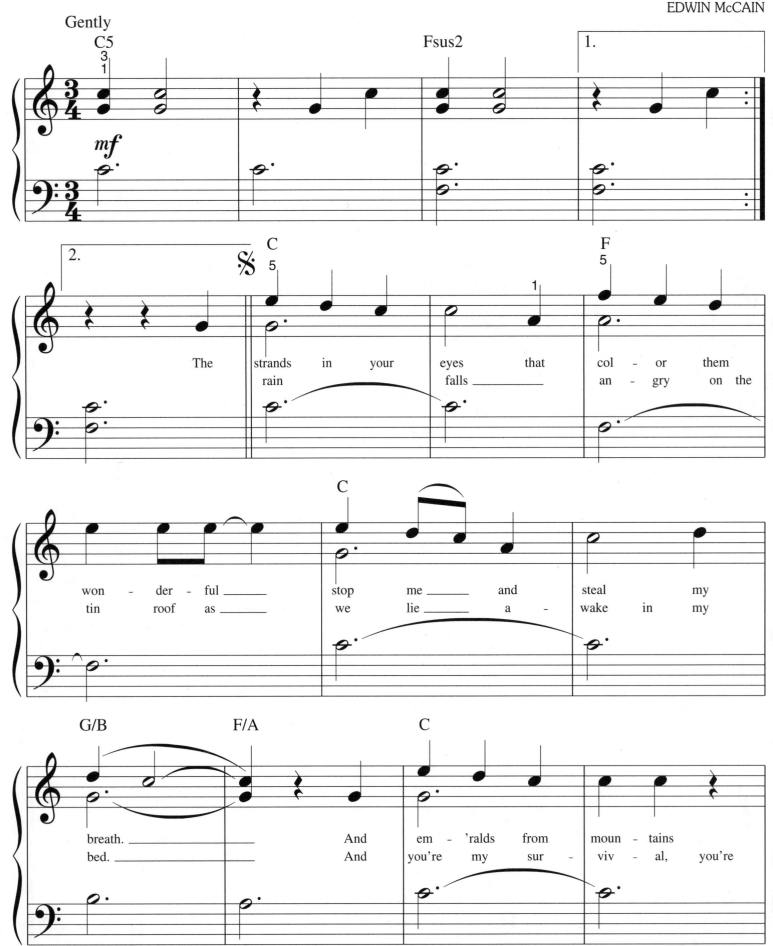

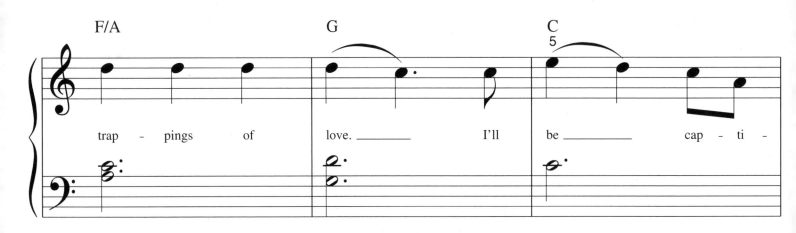

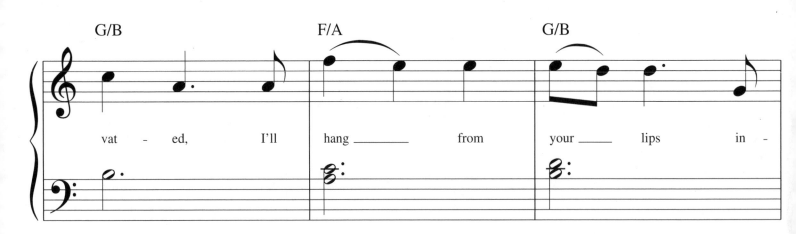

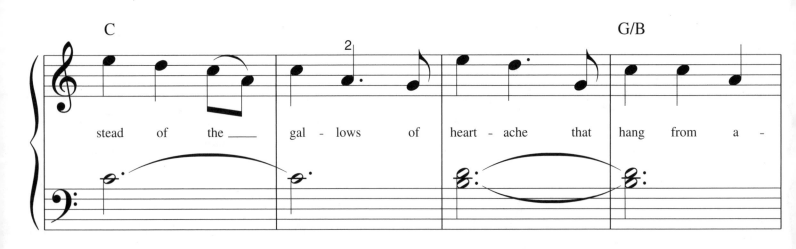

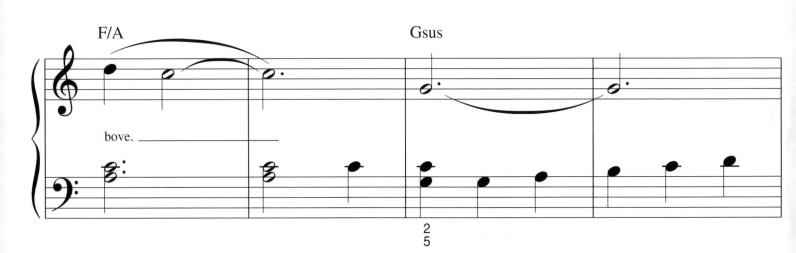

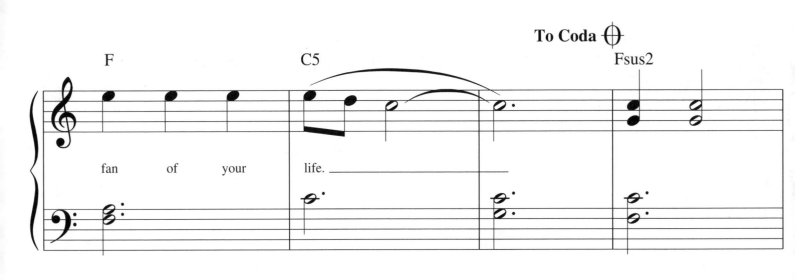

To Coda ⊕

F   C5   Fsus2

fan   of   your   life.

C   G/B   F/A   **D.S. al Coda**

And

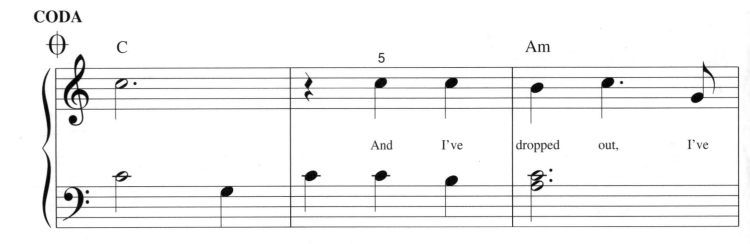

CODA

⊕   C   5   Am

And   I've   dropped   out,   I've

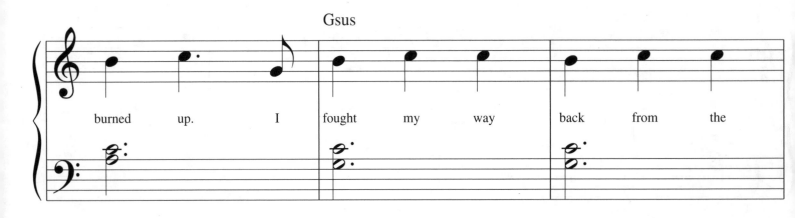

Gsus

burned   up.   I   fought   my   way   back   from   the

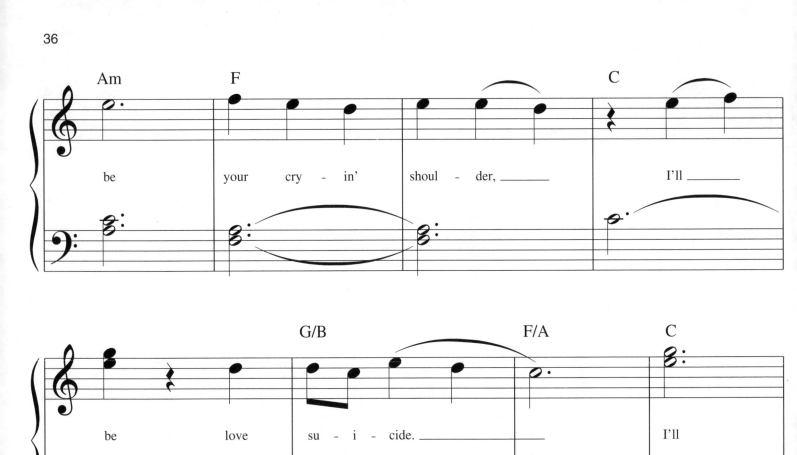

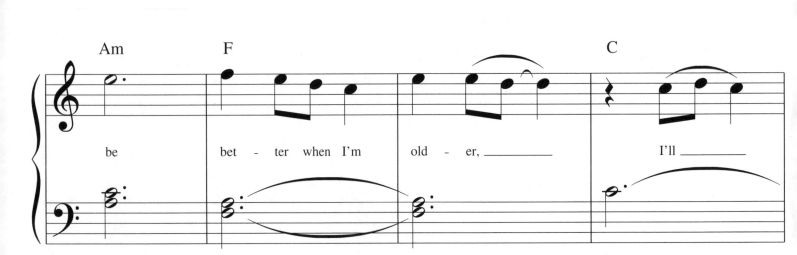

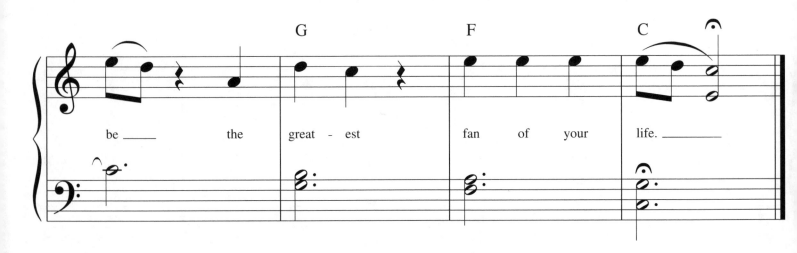

IRIS
from the Motion Picture CITY OF ANGELS

Words and Music by
JOHN RZEZNIK

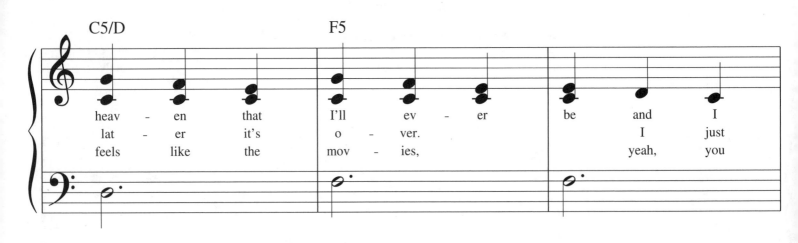

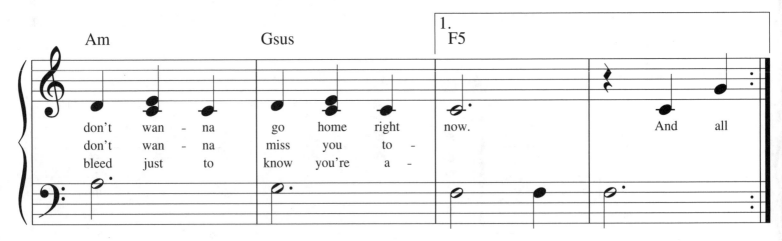

stand.

When ev - 'ry - thing's made to be

bro - ken

I just want you to know who I am.

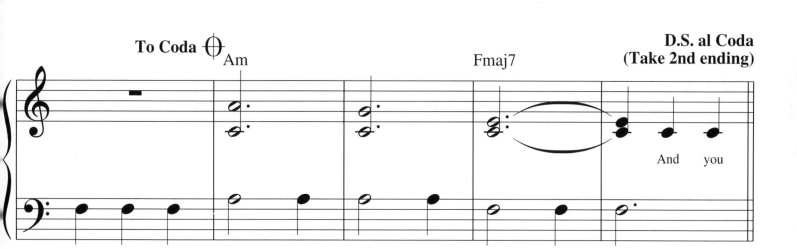

To Coda ⊕ Am

D.S. al Coda
(Take 2nd ending)

Fmaj7

And you

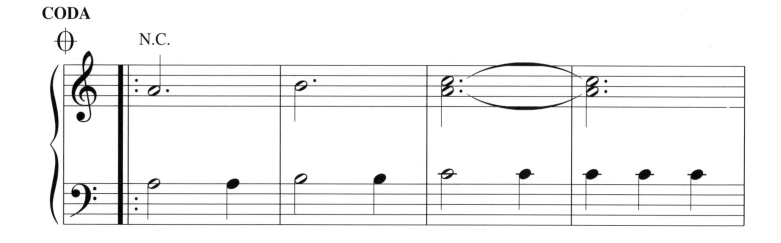

CODA

⊕

N.C.

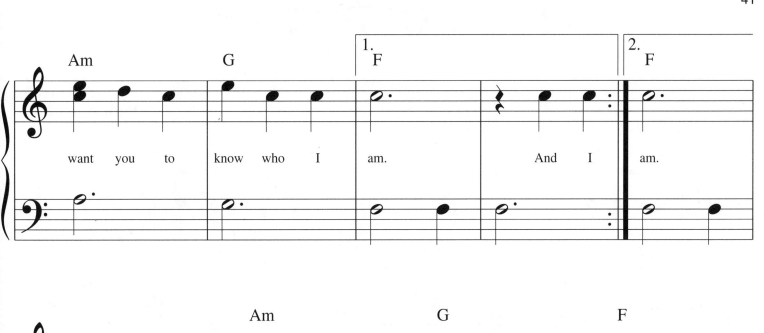

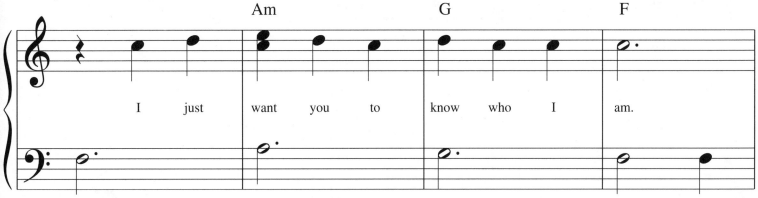

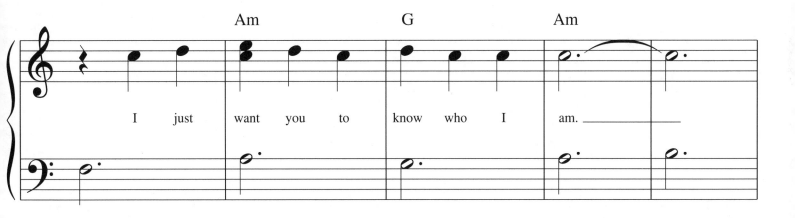

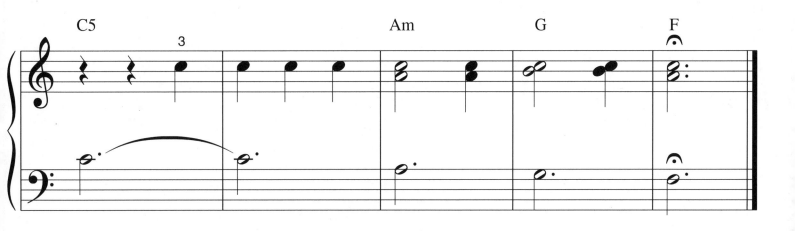

IT'S YOUR LOVE

Words and Music by
STEPHONY E. SMITH

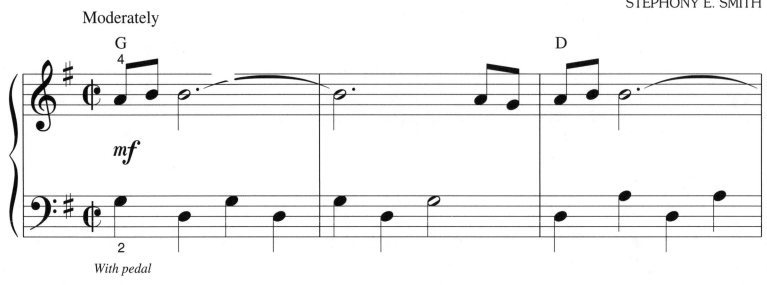

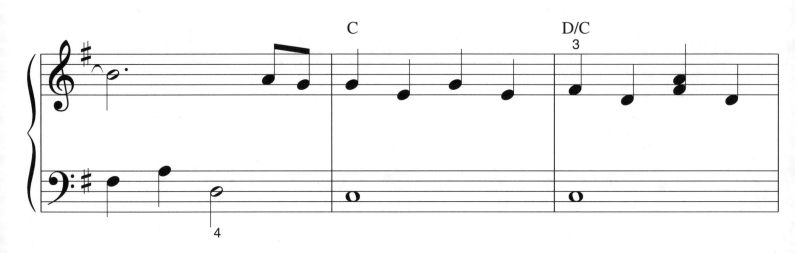

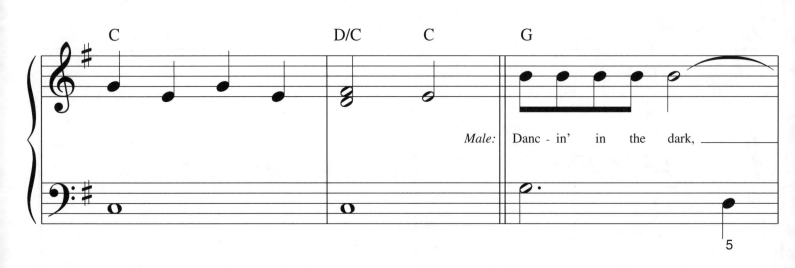

Male: Danc - in' in the dark, _____

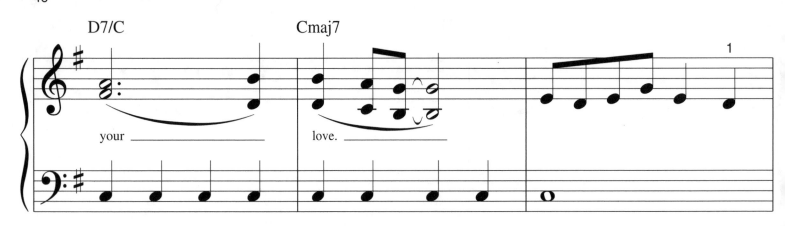

your _____ love. _____

Male: Bet - ter than I was, _____ more than I am, _____

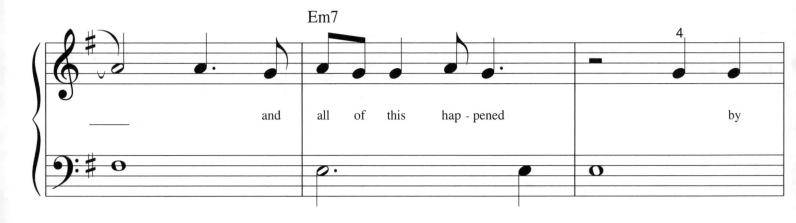

_____ and all of this hap - pened by

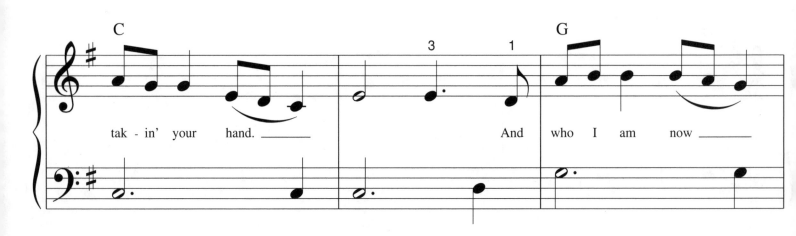

tak - in' your hand. _____ And who I am now _____

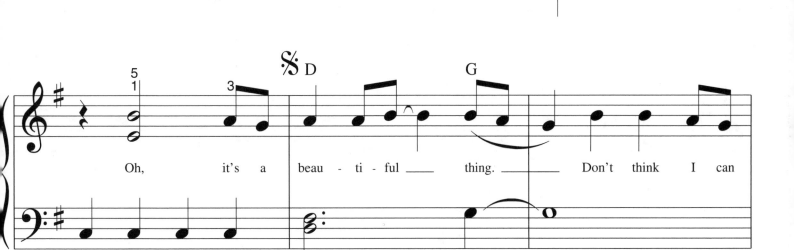

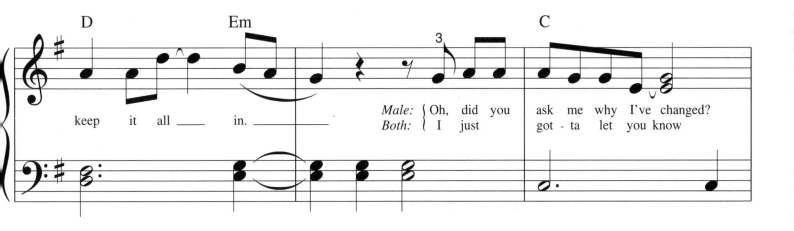

MY HEART WILL GO ON

(Love Theme from 'Titanic')

from the Paramount and Twentieth Century Fox Motion Picture TITANIC

Music by JAMES HORNER
Lyric by WILL JENNINGS

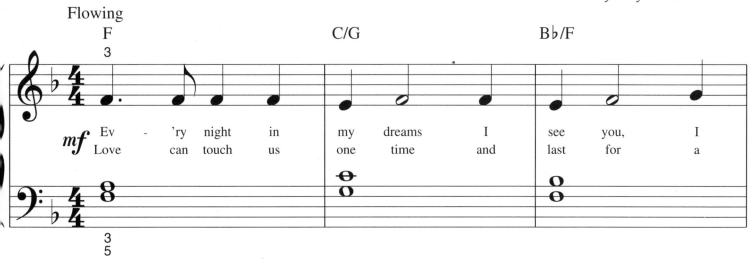

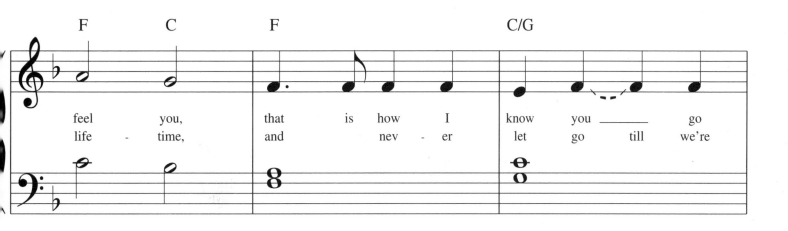

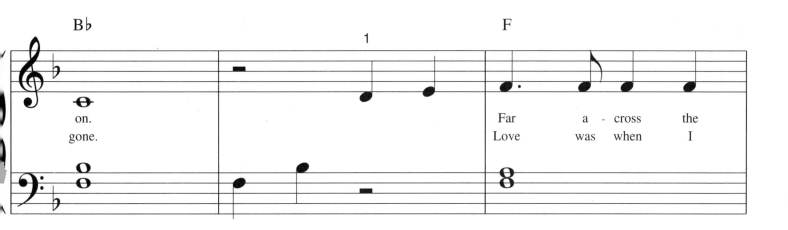

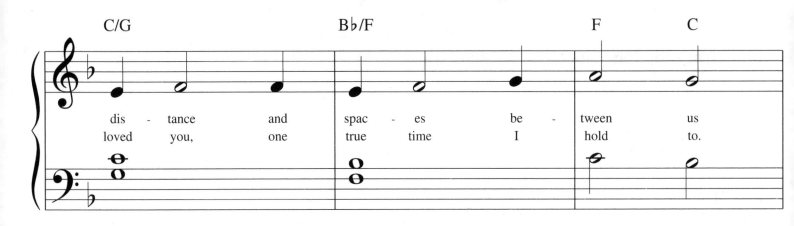

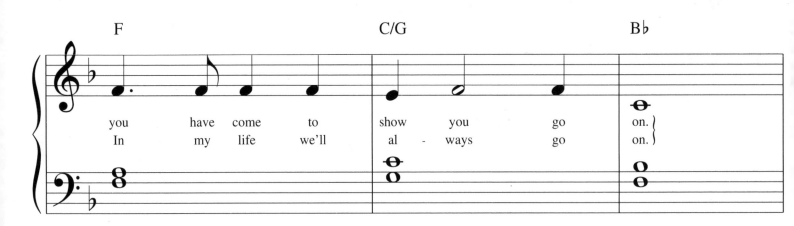

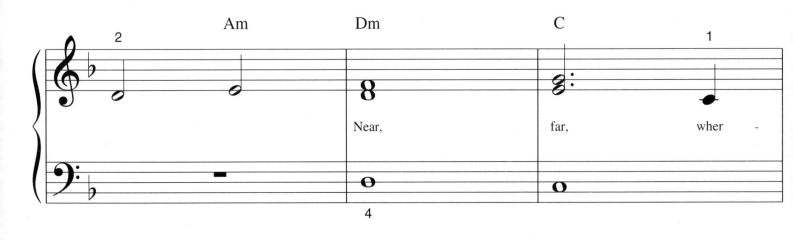

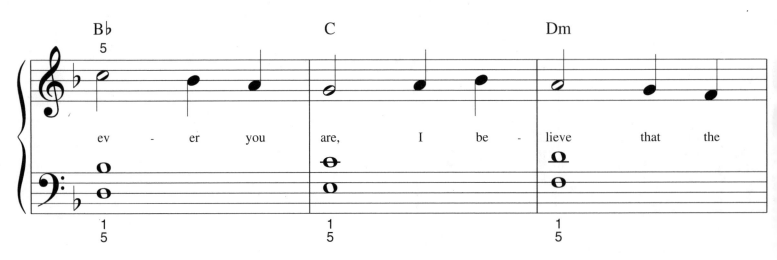

MAMBO NO. 5
(A Little Bit Of...)

Original Music by DAMASO PEREZ PRADO
Words by LOU BEGA and ZIPPY

D.S. al Coda

CODA

looks like this then you're do - in' it right.
A lit - tle bit of
A lit - tle bit of
Mon - i - ca in my life, ___ a lit - tle bit of
Er - i - ca by my side, ___ a lit - tle bit of

MY FATHER'S EYES

Words and Music by
ERIC CLAPTON

REFLECTION

from Walt Disney Pictures' MULAN

Music by MATTHEW WILDER
Lyrics by DAVID ZIPPEL

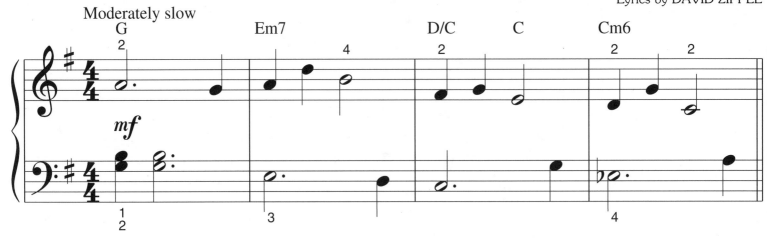

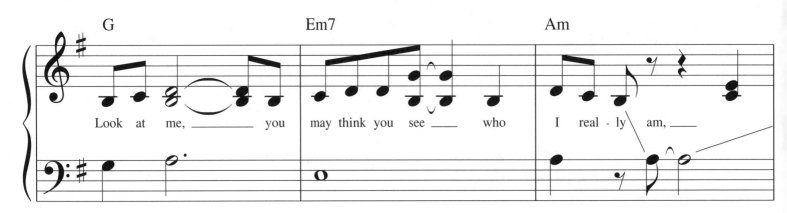

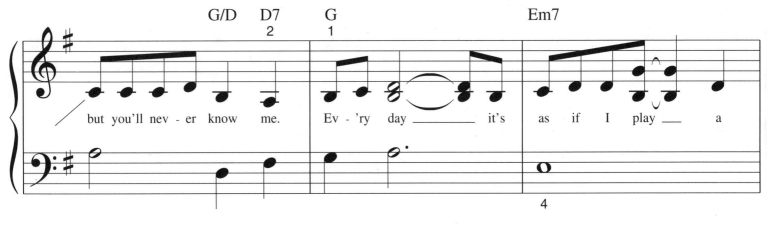

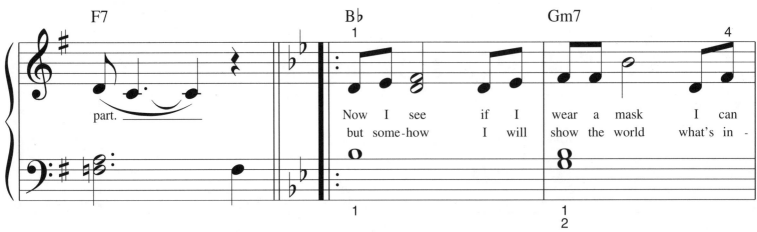

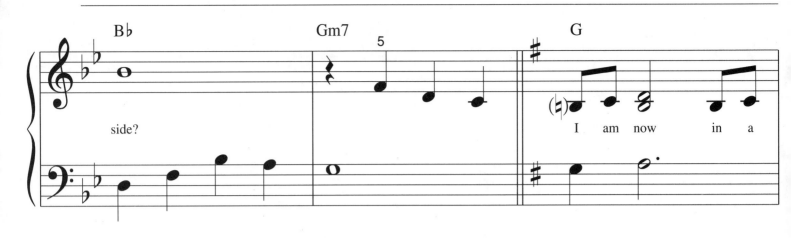

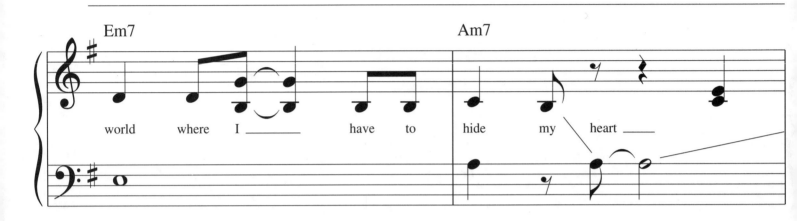

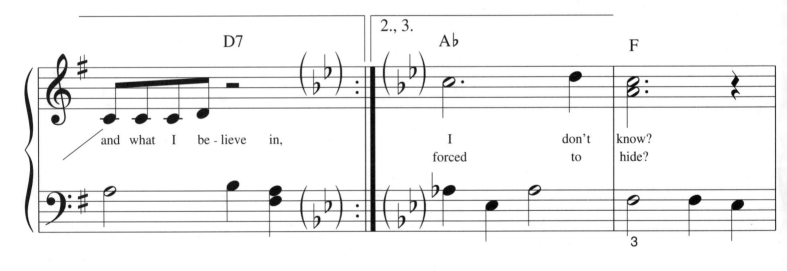

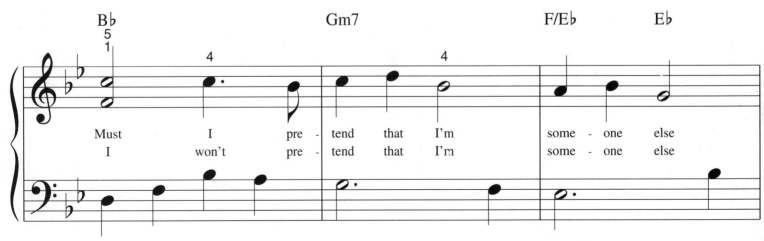

To Coda ⊕

for all time? When will my re - flec - tion show
for all time. When will my re - flec - tion show

who I am?____ In - side, ___ there's a heart that must be

free to fly, that burns with a

D.S. al Coda
(take 2nd ending)

need to know the rea - son _____ why.

TO LOVE YOU MORE

Words and Music by DAVID FOSTER
and JUNIOR MILES

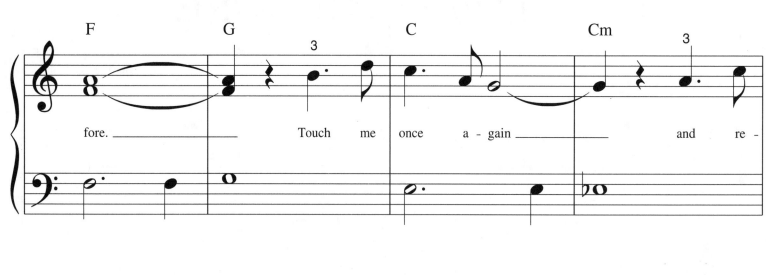

F   G   C   Cm

fore. _____ Touch me once a - gain _____ and re -

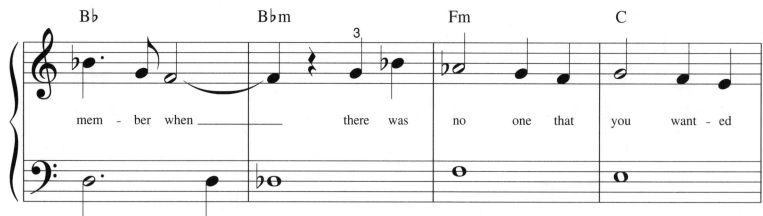

Bb   Bbm   Fm   C

mem - ber when _____ there was no one that you want - ed

Gsus   G   C

more.   Don't go,   you __ know you'll
                 See me   as __ if you

G   Am

break my heart. _____ She won't
nev - er know. _____ Hold me

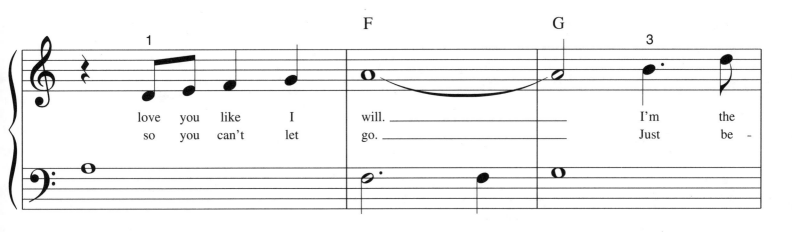

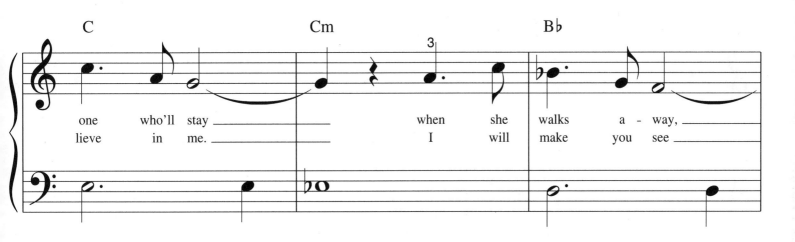

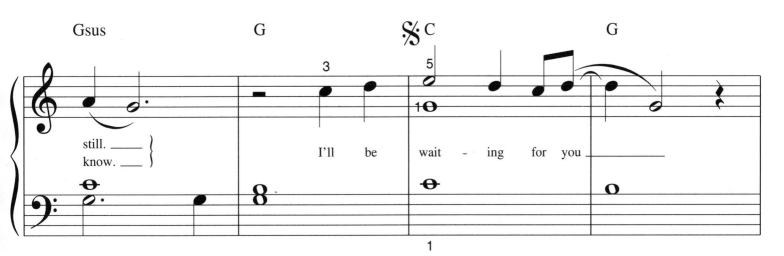

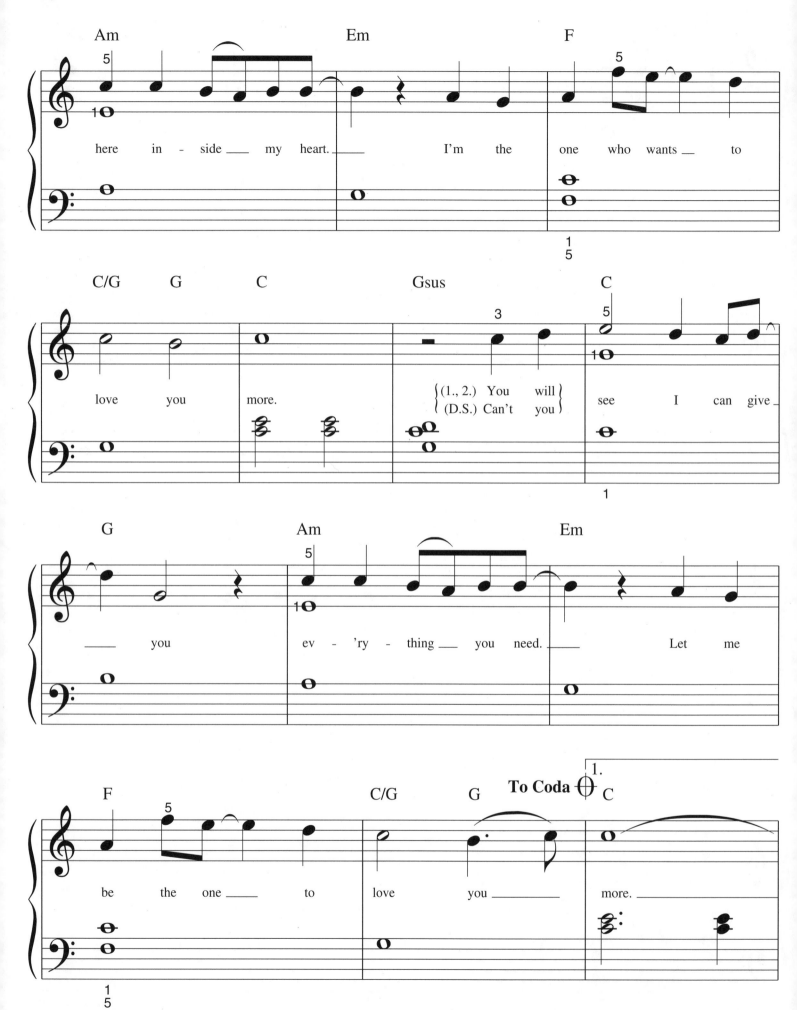

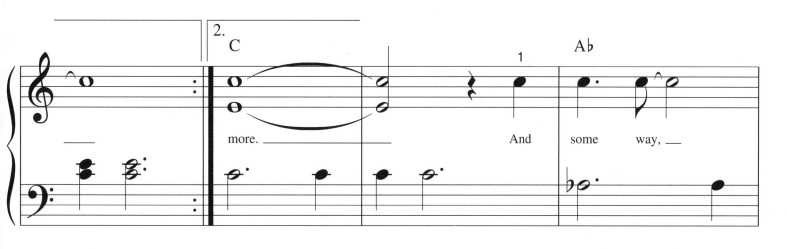

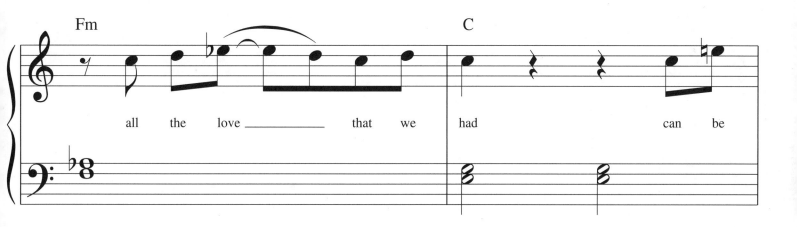

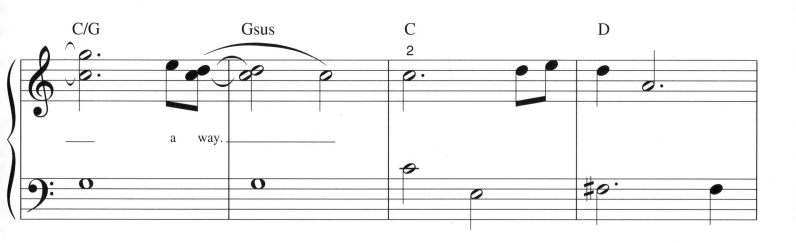

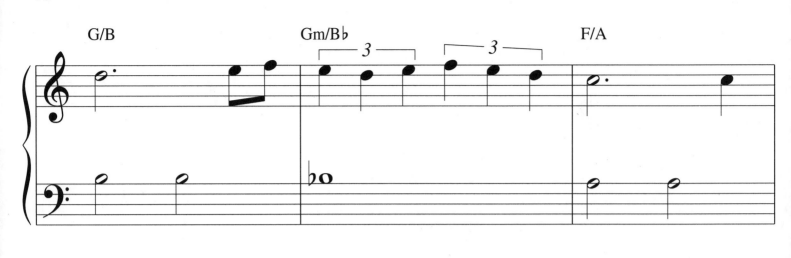

Be - lieve in me. I will

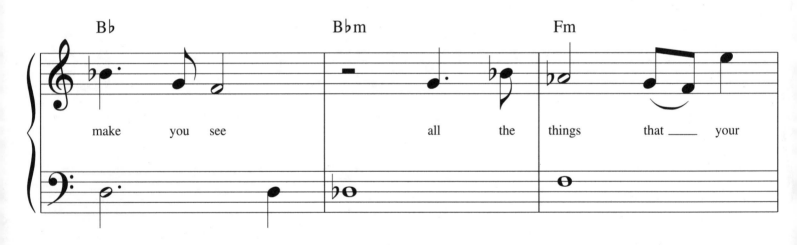

make you see all the things that ___ your

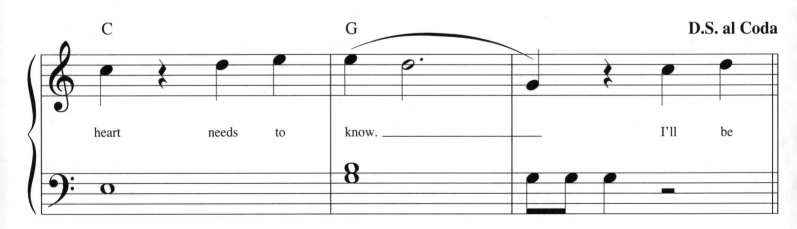

heart needs to know. _____ I'll be

VALENTINE

Words and Music by JACK KUGELL
and JIM BRICKMAN

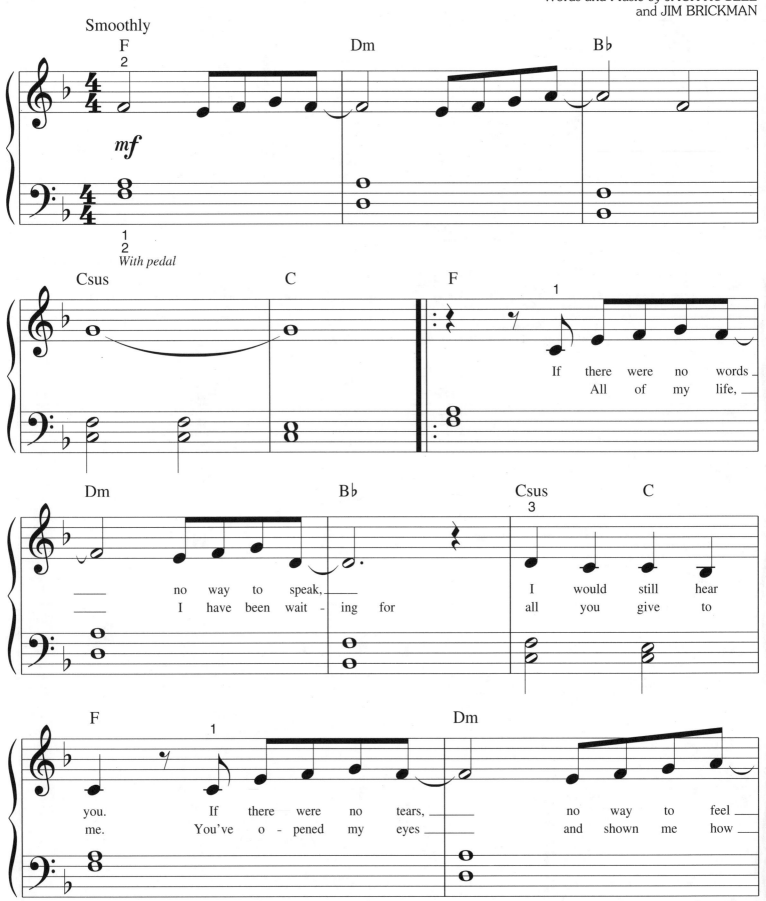

still have my heart ___ un - til the end of time. _____ 'Cause

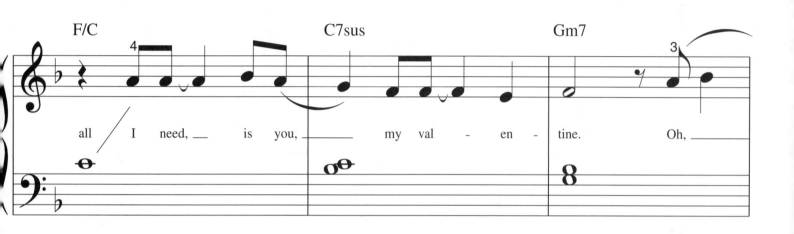

all / I need, ___ is you, _____ my val - en - tine. Oh, _____

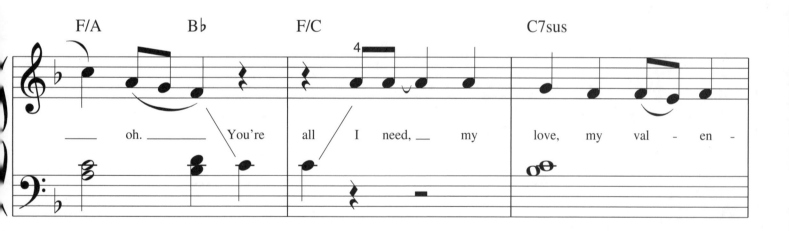

___ oh. _____ You're all / I need, ___ my love, my val - en -

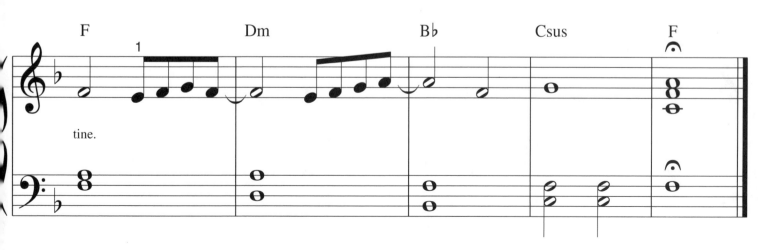

tine.

YOU'LL BE IN MY HEART

(Pop Version)
from Walt Disney Pictures' TARZAN™

Words and Music by
PHIL COLLINS

Moderately, in "2"

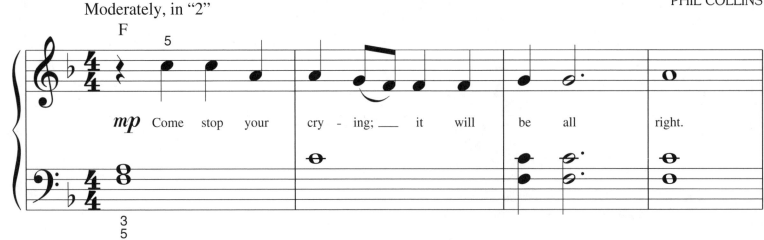

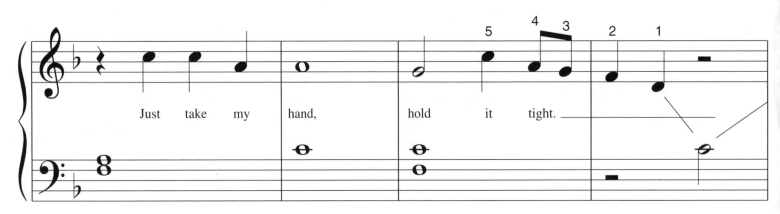

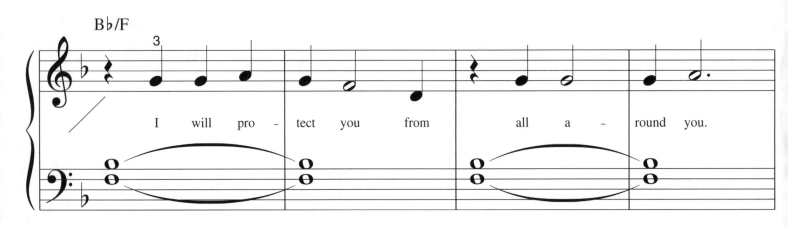

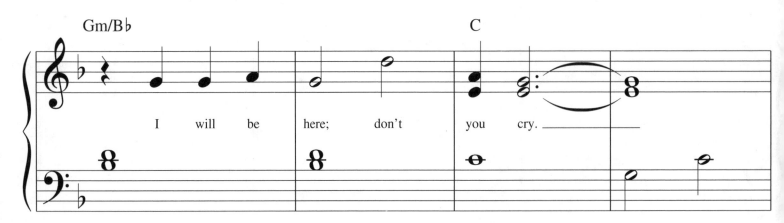

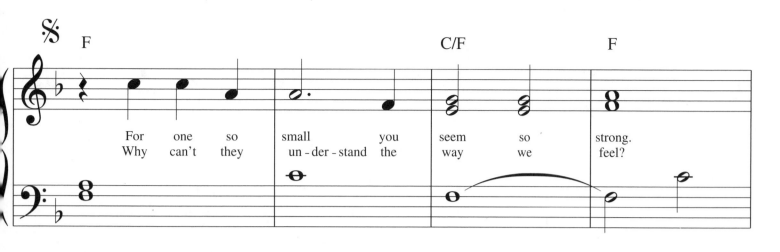

For one so small you seem so strong.
Why can't they un-der-stand the way we feel?

My arms will hold you, ___ keep you safe and
They just won't trust _____ what they can't ex -

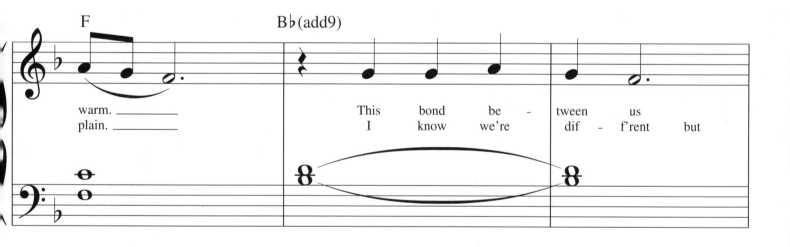

warm. _____
plain. _____

This bond be - tween us
I know we're dif - f'rent but

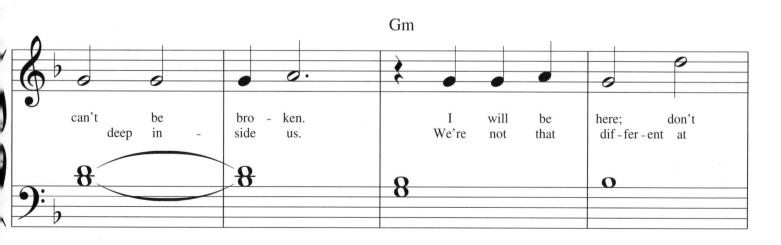

can't be bro - ken.
deep in - side us.

I will be here; don't
We're not that dif - fer - ent at

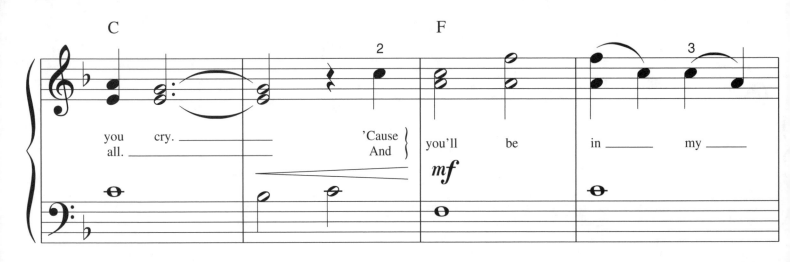

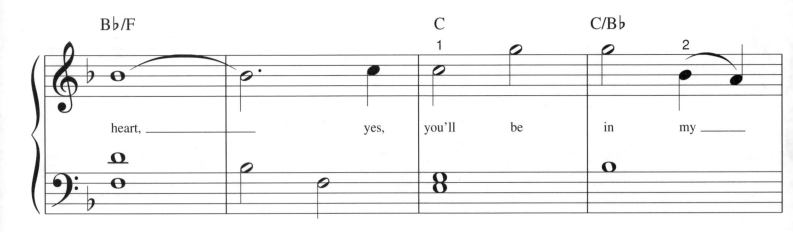

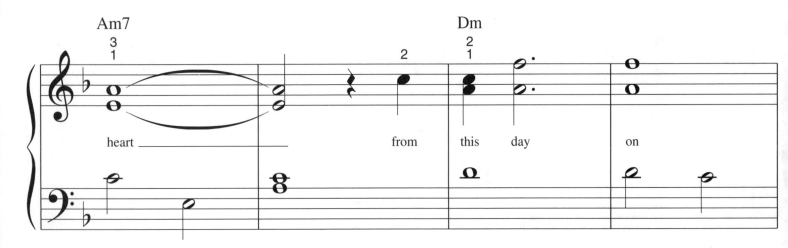

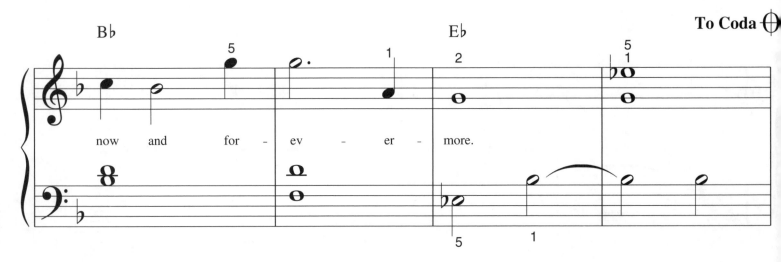

88

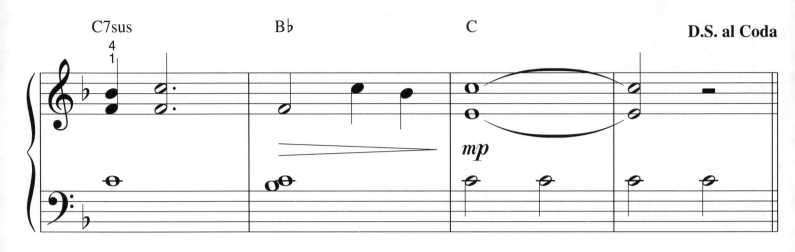

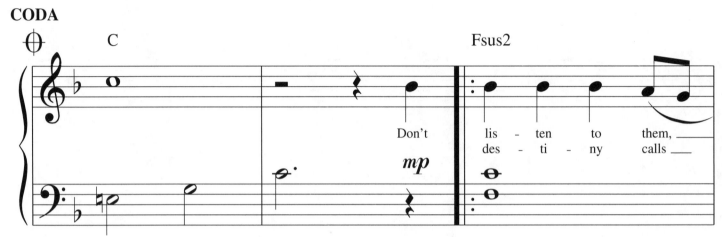

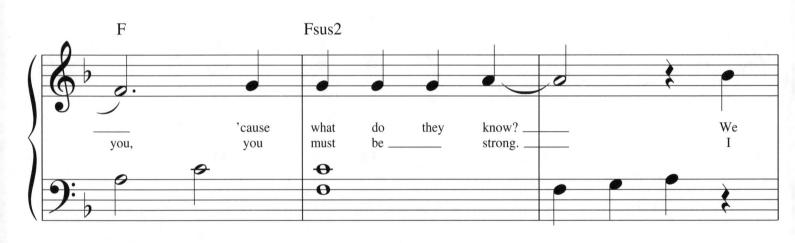

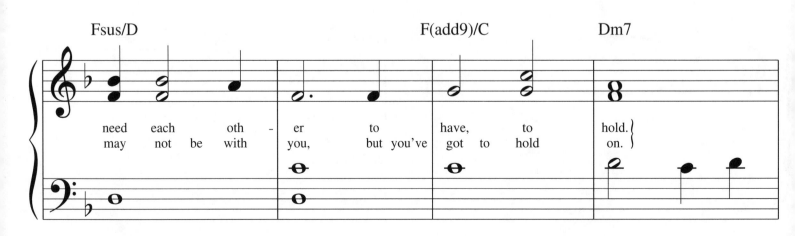

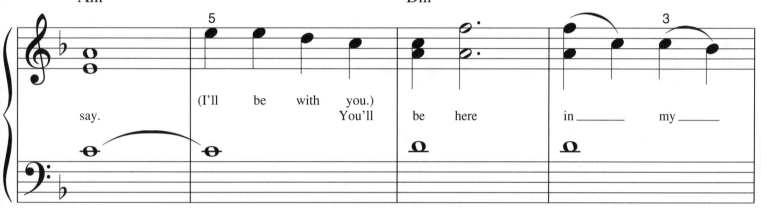

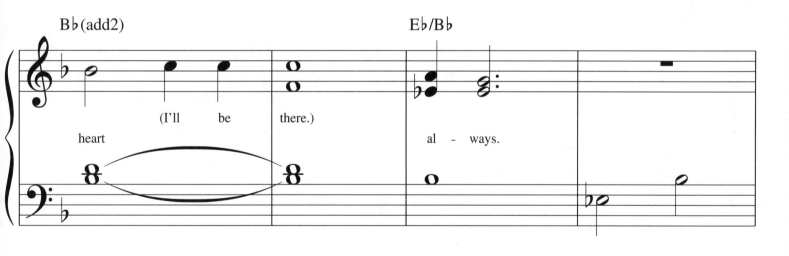

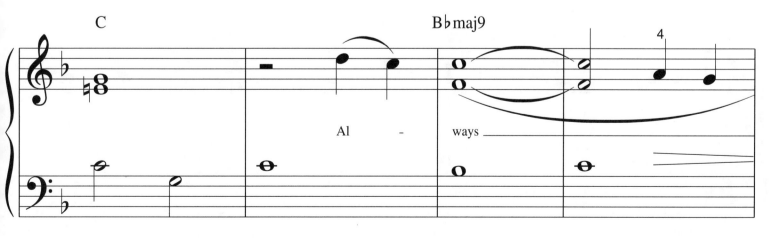

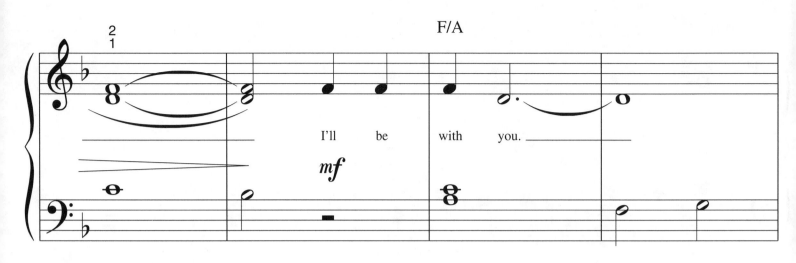

I'll be with you.

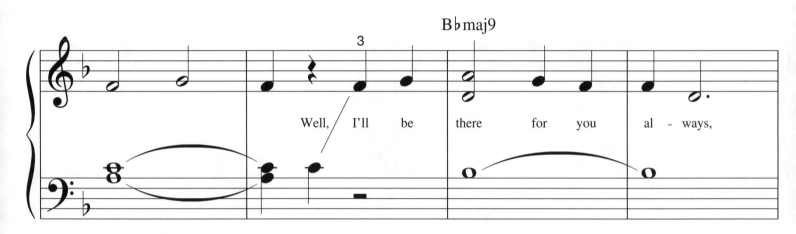

Well, I'll be there for you al - ways,

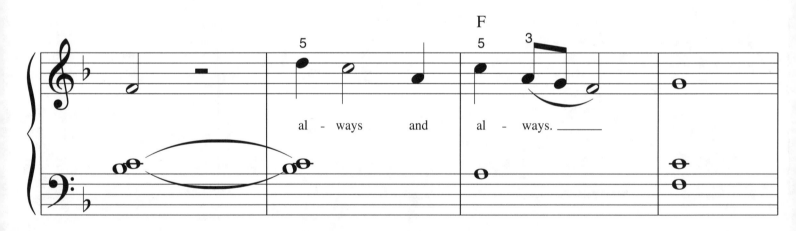

al - ways and al - ways.

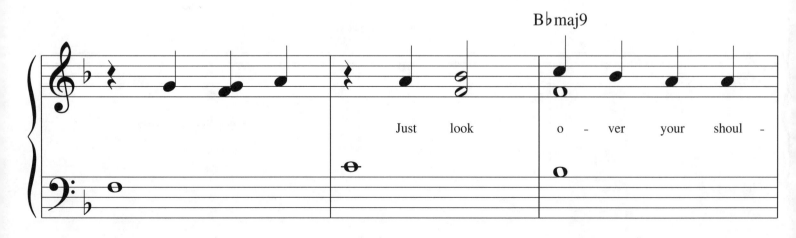

Just look o - ver your shoul -

BIG FUN WITH BIG-NOTE PIANO BOOKS!

These songbooks feature exciting easy arrangements for beginning piano students.

Broadway Classics
Bill Boyd
12 broadway favorites for big note piano, including: Don't Cry for Me Argentina • Give My Regards to Broadway • If I Were a Rich Man • Memory • The Sound of Music • and more.
00290180 ....$7.95

Great Jazz Standards
arranged by Bill Boyd
20 songs, including: April in Paris • Don't Get Around Much Anymore • How High the Moon • It Don't Mean a Thing (If It Ain't Got That Swing) • When I Fall in Love • and more.
00222575 ....$12.95

Broadway Favorites
Bill Boyd
12 Broadway favorites for big-note piano, including: All I Ask of You • Edelweiss • Everything's Coming Up Roses • I Dreamed a Dream • Sunrise, Sunset • and more!
00290184 ....$7.95

Hymn Favorites
Includes 20 favorite hymns: Abide with Me • Blest Be the Tie That Binds • Jesus Loves Me • Nearer My God to Thee • Rock of Ages • What a Friend We Have in Jesus • and more.
00221802 ....$6.95

Children's Favorites
14 songs children love, including: The Brady Bunch • Casper the Friendly Ghost • Going to the Zoo • The Grouch Song • Hakuna Matata • The Name Game • The Siamese Cat Song • Winnie the Pooh • more.
00310282 ....$7.95

Les Misérables
14 songs, including: At the End of the Day • Bring Him Home • Castle On a Cloud • Do You Hear the People Sing • I Dreamed a Dream • In My Life • On My Own • and more.
00221812 ....$12.95

A Christmas Collection
33 simplified favorites, including: The Christmas Song (Chestnuts Roasting) • Frosty the Snow Man • A Holly Jolly Christmas • I Saw Mommy Kissing Santa Claus • Mister Santa • The Most Wonderful Day of the Year • Nuttin' for Christmas • Silver Bells • and more.
00221818 ....$10.95

Disney's Tarzan
8 great Phil Collins tunes from the animated Disney hit: Son of Man • Strangers like Me • Trashin' the Camp • Two Worlds • Two Worlds (Finale) • Two Worlds (Reprise) • You'll Be in My Heart • You'll Be in My Heart (Pop Version).
00316049 ....$12.95

Classical Music's Greatest Hits
24 beloved classical pieces including: Air on the G String • Ave Maria • By the Beautiful Blue Danube • Canon in D • Eine Kleine Nachtmusik • Für Elise • Ode to Joy • Romeo and Juliet • Waltz of the Flowers • more.
00310475 ....$9.95

Movie Hits
21 songs popularized on the silver screen, including: Beauty and the Beast • Don't Worry Be Happy • Endless Love • The Rainbow Connection • Somewhere Out There • Tears in Heaven • Unchained Melody • Under the Sea • A Whole New World • and more.
00221804 ....$9.95

Country Favorites
28 songs, including: Achy Breaky Heart • Down at the Twist & Shout • God Bless the U.S.A. • Your Cheatin' Heart • and more.
00222554 ....$10.95

Patriotic Gems
arr. Bill Boyd
20 American classics, including: America • America, The Beautiful • Battle Hymn of the Republic • Semper Fidelis • Star Spangled Banner • You're a Grand Old Flag • and more.
00221801 ....$6.95

Disney Movie Magic
Big-note arrangements of 12 Disney movie songs: Arabian Nights • Beauty and the Beast • Circle of Life • Colors of the Wind • God Help the Outcasts • Hakuna Matata • Kiss the Girl • Part of Your World • Someday • Something There • A Whole New World • more.
00310194 ....$10.95

TV Hits
Over 20 theme songs that everyone knows, including: Brady Bunch • Cheers • (Meet) The Flintstones • Home Improvement • The Jetsons • Northern Exposure • Mr. Ed • The Munsters Theme • Won't You Be My Neighbor • and more fun favorites!
00221805 ....$9.95

Prices, contents, and availability subject to change without notice.
Disney artwork © Disney Enterprises, Inc.

FOR MORE INFORMATION, SEE YOUR LOCAL MUSIC DEALER,
OR WRITE TO:

HAL•LEONARD®
CORPORATION

7777 W. BLUEMOUND RD. P.O. BOX 13819 MILWAUKEE, WI 53213
www.halleonard.com

0100

It's Easy to Play Your Favorite Songs with Hal Leonard Easy Piano Books